No More Minutes

The story of two little boys who always want more time before bed.

HUDSON & GRANT BIBERAJ

Archway Publishing books may be ordered through booksellers or by contacting:

Archway Publishing
1663 Liberty Drive
Bloomington, IN 47403
www.archwaypublishing.com
844-669-3957

Author cover photo: Sohale Razmjou Photography

ISBN: 978-1-6657-4409-6 (sc)
ISBN: 978-1-6657-4411-9 (hc)
ISBN: 978-1-6657-4410-2 (e)

Library of Congress Control Number: 2023908978

Print information available on the last page.

Archway Publishing rev. date: 05/19/2023

To our baby sister, Lucy, there are always a few minutes before bedtime. You just have to find the right way to ask for them.

Boys, time for bed.

Can we play for 5 more minutes?

No more minutes, time for bed.

How about 7 more minutes?

Huh? No more minutes, time for bed.

Dad, can we play a game?

No more games, time for bed.

Can we play Croc-O-Monster?

No Croc-O-Monster, time for bed.

Can we read a book?

No more books, time for bed.

Can we read 5 more books?

No more books, time for bed.

Can you tell us a story?

No more stories, time for bed.

I'm hungry, can we have a snack?

No more snacks, go to bed.

Actually, can we have an apple?

Apple? No more apples, go to bed.

I have to go to bathroom.

No more bathroom, go to bed.

—quiet—

What if I have a nightmare?

No more nightmares, go to bed.

Can I call my cousins?

What?! No more cousins, no more calls, go to bed.

—quieter—

Dad, why do they call a door, a door?

What?! No more doors, go to bed.

16

Dad, we love baby sister.

Good. I love baby sister too.

Can we kiss baby sister good night?

No more kisses, go to bed.

Can you scratch my back?

No more back scratching, go to bed.

Dad....

No....

I love you...

.....I love you.

I love you to infinity.

Fine. Five more minutes.

Dad, can we go downstairs?

5 more minutes

NO MORE MINUTES! Time to wake up!

Printed in the United States
by Baker & Taylor Publisher Services